SAUDI SECURITIES LAW DICTIONARY

MICHAEL O'KANE

ISBN:

(ePub): 978-1-945979-26-2

(Print): 978-1-945979-27-9

✽ Created with Vellum

INTRODUCTION

This dictionary is based on the Saudi Capital Markets Authority's *Amended Glossary of Defined Terms*[1] with additions of defined terms as found in the thirty-six other Saudi securities laws. The Amended Glossary is unfortunately, in no way comprehensive. Definitions are found throughout the other thirty-six laws, usually, but not always, at the beginning of each legal text. Given that some of these laws are in excess of one hundred pages and even contain their own tables of contents, it is not altogether surprising that the draftsmen of each law would take it upon themselves to draft their own list of terms which play a prominent role in their discrete legislative work.

A more comprehensive work was needed, one bringing all the definitions together in one place. This dictionary modestly proposes to fill this need.

The dictionary is a companion text to the single volume *Saudi Securities Laws*, a comprehensive collection of all Saudi securities laws.

Michael O'Kane
November, 2022

A

Accounting Firm: The entity which carries on audit engagements in accordance with the provisions of the Law of Certified Public Accountants, whether it is an individual or professional firm.Art.2(c), Registration of Auditors

Accounts: are to be read to include any business relationships between Authorized Person and its client. Art 2, AML Regulations

Accredited Valuer: A legal or natural person licensed to carry out the valuation profession in accordance with the Accredited Valuers Law issued by Royal Decree no.(M/43) dated 9/7/1433H. and its implementing regulation (Real-Estate Valuation Sector).

Accumulated Losses: The company's results for the current period added to the company's accumulated results from prior periods, which in aggregate represent a loss, and appear as a separate item under shareholder's equity on the balance sheet.Art. 1, Procedures for Listed Companies with Losses

Acting in Concert: means, at the sole discretion of the Authority, actively co-operating, pursuant to an agreement (whether binding or non-binding) or an understanding (whether formal or informal) between persons, to be controllers (whether directly or indirectly, excluding indirect ownership of shares through swap agreements or through an investment fund whose unit owner have no discretion in its investment decisions) of a company, through the acquisition by any of them (through direct or indirect ownership) of voting shares in that company. Moreover, "concert parties" shall be construed accordingly. Without prejudice to the general application of this definition, the following persons, shall be presumed to be acting in concert with other persons of the same class unless the contrary is established, including but not be limited to:

1. Members of the same group;

2. a person's relatives;

3. Person(s) who provided financial assistance to the offeror or offer, or members of the group with such person (other than a bank in the ordinary course of business) in order to purchase shares that carry voting rights or convertible debt instruments.

Acting in Concert: means in the Rules on the Offer of Securities and Continuing Obligations, actively co-operating, pursuant to an agreement or understanding (whether formal or informal) between persons, to acquire interest in or exercise voting right in the shares or in the convertible debt instruments of the issuer.

Administrative Team: A group of individuals

who make strategic decisions of the person. The Board is the Company's Administrative Team. Art 1, Corporate Governance Regulations

Advising: advising a person in relation to a security, including advising on the merits of dealing in it, exercising any right to deal conferred by it or financial planning and wealth management in it.

Affiliate: a person who controls another person or is controlled by that other person, or who is under common control with that person by a third person. In any of the preceding, control could be direct or indirect.

Anti-Money Laundering Law: the Anti-Money Laundering Law issued by Royal Decree No. M/20 dated 5/2/1439 H.

Applicant: a foreign investor that submits an application for qualification to an assessing authorized person. Art. 2(c), Qualified Foreign Financial Institutions Regulations

Application for Listing: means in the Rules on the Offer of Securities and Continuing Obligations, any application submitted to the Exchange to list securities of any type.

Application for Registration and Offer: the registration of securities with the Authority, or where the context permits, the application to the Authority for registration and offer of securities.

Appeal Panel: the appeal panel formed pursuant to paragraph (g) of Article 25 of the Capital Markets Law. Art. 1, Securities Disputes Proceedings Regulations

Appropriate Close-out Period: the time period to close all open positions of the defaulting

Clearing Member which starts from the last collateral provided by the defaulted clearing member until the closing of his positions. Article 2, Securities Central Counterparts Regulations

Arranging: introducing parties in relation to offering of securities, arrangement of its underwriting, or advising on corporate finance business.

Assessing Authorized Person: an Authorized Person who has agreed with an applicant to assess its application for registration as a QFI, or an authorized person who has executed a QFI assessment agreement with a QFI. Art. 2(c), Qualified Foreign Financial Institutions Regulations

Asset-Backed Debt Instrument: means a debt instrument issued by a special purposes entity under whose terms: (a) the entitlement of holders of the debt instrument to a return is wholly dependent on the returns generated by the special purposes entity's assets; and (b) the sponsor is not obliged to the holders of the debt instrument (whether by guarantee or otherwise) to pay any amounts due on the debt instrument.

Asset-Linked Recourse Debt Instrument: means a debt instrument issued by a special purposes entity under whose terms: (a) the entitlement of holders of the debt instrument to a return is defined by a percentage of the returns generated by the special purposes entity's assets; and (b) the sponsor is obliged to the holders of the debt instrument (whether by guarantee or otherwise) to pay all amounts due on the debt instrument.

Associate:

1) in relation to the senior executives or a director or to a substantial shareholder who is an individual any of the following:

(a) that individual's spouse or minor children (together "the individual's family"); and

(b) any company in whose equity shares the individual or any member or members (taken together) of the individual's family or the individual and any such member or members (taken together) are directly or indirectly interested so that they are able:

(i) to exercise or control the exercise of 30% or more of the votes at the general meeting on all, or substantially all, matters; or

(ii) to appoint or remove directors holding a majority of voting rights at board meetings on all, or substantially all, matters; and

2) in relation to a substantial shareholder which is a company:

(a) any other company which is its subsidiary or parent or fellow subsidiary of the parent;

(b) any company whose directors are accustomed to act in accordance with the substantial shareholder's directions or instructions; and

(c) any company in the capital of which the substantial shareholder, and any other company under (a) or (b) taken together, are directly or indirectly interested so that they are able:

(i) to exercise or control the exercise of 30% or more of the votes at the general meeting on all, or substantially all, matters; or

(ii) to appoint or remove directors holding a majority of voting rights at board meetings on all, or substantially all, matters.

Attachment: shall mean the provisional ban on transferring, exchanging, disposing with or moving funds and proceeds or attaching same pursuant to an order by a court or a competent authority. Art.2, AML Regs.

Audit Engagements: Audit of financial statements, prepared by an entity, in accordance with the auditing standards adopted by the Saudi Organization for Certified Public Accountants for the purpose of expressing an opinion as to whether such financial statements present fairly the financial position of the entity at a specific date, and the results of its operations for a specific financial period, or review of the interim financial statements, prepared by the entity, to determine if significant amendments are needed for the interim financial statements to be in agreement with the accounting standards adopted by the Saudi Organization for Certified Public Accountants. Art.2(c), Registration of Auditors

Authorized Credit Rating Agency: a legal person which is incorporated, and authorized, in the Kingdom to carry out rating activities in accordance with the Credit Rating Agencies Regulations or an authorized foreign credit rating agency.

Authorization Requirement: the authorization requirement as stated in Article (5) of the Securities Business Regulations. i.e., a person must not carry on securities business in the Kingdom unless he is...a Capital Market Institution authorised by the Authority; Art. 2(c), Qualified Foreign Financial Institutions Regulations.

Authorized Foreign Credit Rating Agency: a

foreign credit rating agency authorized to carry out rating activities in the Kingdom in accordance with the Credit Rating Agencies Regulations.

Authorized Person: means a Capital Market Institution.

Authorized Persons Regulations: means the Capital Market Institutions Regulations issued by the Board of the Capital Market Authority.

Authority: the Capital Market Authority, including where the context permits any committee, sub-committee, employee or agent to whom any function of the Authority may be delegated.

B

Backtesting: an ex-post comparison of observed outcomes with expected outcomes derived from the use of margin models. Article 2, Securities Central Counterparts Regulations

Bank: a financial institution that has a legal personality which engages in banking business. Art. 2(c), Qualified Foreign Financial Institutions Regulations

Bankruptcy Regulations: the Bankruptcy Law issued by Royal Decree No. M/50 dated 28/5/1439H. or any applicable provisions relating to insolvency or bankruptcy under the Companies Regulations, or any other legislation dealing with bankruptcy issues in the Kingdom.

Beneficiary: for the purposes of the Rules for the Special Purposes Entities, means: the person for which the special purposes entity is established to provide such a person with the necessary financing by issuing debt instruments, in accordance with the provisions of the Rules for the Special Purposes Entities. Art. 2(d), Direct Financing Investment Funds Instructions

Beneficial Owner: refers to the natural person(s) who ultimately own(s) or control(s) the funds of the clients or on whose behalf a transaction or activity is being conducted. It also incorporates those persons who exercise ultimate effective control over a legal person or arrangement. Art.2, AML, see, "Ultimate beneficiary."

Bidding Application (Appended): The application submitted to the financial advisor of the issuer when the price range is changed, in accordance with paragraph (b) of Part (4) of these Instructions, in time no later than the last day of the Book building period, and submitted by participating parties in order to participate in the book building or by the participating entities for the purpose of changing their requests concerning the price range. Art. 2(c), IPO Book Building

Book Building: The process by which a financial advisor registers bids from participating entities in order to determine the offering price. Art. 2(c), IPO Book Building

Book Building Period: A period determined by the financial advisor, after obtaining the consent of the issuer, without prejudice to paragraph (d) of Part (3) of these Instructions. It starts from the first day of the financial advisor offering the issuer's shares to the participating entities in accordance with paragraph (a) of Part (3) of these Instructions. Art. 2(c), IPO Book Building

Bidding Participation Application: The application submitted by the participating entities to the financial advisor of the issuer in order to participate in the book building process, and submitted to the financial advisor in time no later than the last day of the book building period. Art. 2(c), IPO Book Building

Brokerage and securities firm: a financial institution that has a legal personality which engages in securities business, including portfolio managers. Art. 2(c), Qualified Foreign Financial Institutions Regulations

Brokerage Professional: an employee of a Capital Market Institution who performs the activity of dealing on behalf of a Capital Market Institution.

Business relationship: means professional or commercial relationship between an Authorized Person and a client. A relationship need not involve the Authorized Person in an actual transaction; giving advice shall also constitute establishing a business relationship. Art. 2, AML Regs.

Buys or Buying: includes buying a security or commodity for consideration.

C

Calendar Day: any day, whether or not such day is a business day.

Capital Base: comprised of Tier-1 capital and Tier-2 capital. Art. 1(f), Prudential Rules

Capital Market Institution: a person authorized by the Authority to carry out securities business.

Capital Market Institutions Regulations: the Capital Market Institutions Regulations issued by the Board of the Capital Market Authority.

Capital Market Law: the Capital Market Law issued by Royal Decree No. M/30 dated 2/6/1424H.

Capital Protected Fund: an investment fund whose primary investment objective is to protect and return the capital invested by unitholders at a pre-determined date in the future.

Capitalization Issue: an offer of further shares to existing shareholders, fully paid up out of the issuer's reserves, in proportion to existing shareholders holdings.

Carve Out: is a type of Demerger transaction where the Listed Company sells off a portion of its assets, business or a subsidiary by transferring them as a whole, to one or several existing entities (acquiring legal entities) or to be newly formed, or to the public in return for cash or shares in the acquiring legal entity being granted to the Listed Company.

CCP: a central counterparty authorized in carrying out Securities Clearing activities in the Kingdom in accordance with the Capital Market Law and the Securities Central Counterparties Regulations.

CCP Rules: the regulations, rules, procedures and instructions proposed by the Board of Directors of the CCP and approved by the Board of the Authority.

CDD: An acronym for "Customer Due Diligence."

Center or Depositary Center: the Securities Depositary Center to be established in accordance with Article 26 of the Capital Market Law. Pending the establishment of the Depositary Center, any reference to the Depositary Center shall be construed as a reference to the Tadawul Depositary System at Tadawul.

Central Bank: the Saudi Central Bank, also known as SAMA.

CEO: the chief executive officer, being any individual who heads the operations of any person and includes the managing director, the chief executive, the president of the company or equivalent.

Certificates: certificates or other instruments which confer contractual or property rights:

 1. in respect of any shares, debt instruments,

warrants, being a security held by a person (other than the person on whom the rights are conferred by the certificate or instrument); and

2. the transfer of which may be effected without the consent of that person; but excluding any certificates or instruments which confer contractual or ownership rights of the type of the options, futures or the contracts for differences, and excluding any certificate or instrument which confers rights in respect of two or more securities issued by different persons.

Certified Public Accountant (CPA): The natural person who carries on and is responsible for audit engagements, its performance, and signing of audit reports issued by the accounting firm in accordance with the provisions of the Law of Certified Public Accountants. Art.2(c), Registration of Auditors

CFO (Chief Financial Officer): any natural person who manages the financial affairs of any person, whether under the name of chief financial officer or finance manager or equivalent.

Charged person: a person who is charged with violation of any provision related to the public right of the provisions of the Law, its implementing regulations, and the regulations, rules and instructions issued by the Authority and the Exchange. Art. 1, Securities Disputes Proceedings Regulations

Citizens of the Cooperation Council for the Arab States of the Gulf: natural persons who hold citizenship of one of the Cooperation Council for the Arab States of the Gulf countries, or legal persons that (i) the capital of which is majority owned by citizens or governments of the Cooperation Council for the Arab states of the Gulf; and (ii) are holding the citizenship of one of the Cooperation Council for the Arab states of the Gulf countries ,in accordance with the definition set out in the resolution of the Supreme Council of the Cooperation Council for the Arab States of the Gulf in its 15th session approved by the Council of Ministers Resolution Number (16) dated 20/1/1418H. Part 2(a), Foreign Strategic Ownership in Listed Companies; see "GCC Citizens" and "GCC Companies.

Class Action Suit: a suit filed by a group of plaintiffs against one or more defendants, where the group of plaintiffs' suit share the same legal bases, merits and the subject matter of the requests. Any decision made on the case shall affect all of its parties.Art. 1, Securities Disputes Proceedings Regulations.

Class Action Suits Docket: a docket created by the Committee for Class Action Suits. Art. 1, Securities Disputes Proceedings Regulations

Class Tests: the tests set out in Annex 24 of the Rules on the Offer of Securities and Continuing Obligations, which are used to determine whether a transaction constitutes a Demerger requiring shareholders' approval.

Clearing: the process of establishing each party's rights and obligations arising from Securities trading, including the calculation of net obligations, and ensuring that financial instruments or cash are available to secure the exposures arising from such obligations. Article 2, Securities Central Counterparts Regulations

Clearing Member: a Direct Clearing Member or a General Clearing Member. Article 2, Securities Central Counterparts Regulations

Client: a person for whom a Capital Market Institution executes securities transactions. Also, a execution-only customer either natural or legal person and counterparty for whom an Authorized Person executes securities business. Art. 2, AML Regs. Also, "a natural or legal person which: 1) is not a Clearing Member; and 2) has a contractual relationship with a Clearing Member which enables that person to clear its transactions with the CCP." Article 2, Securities Central Counterparts Regulations.

Client Account: an account at a local bank which is in the name of a Capital Market Institution and fulfills the conditions required by the Client Money Rules.

Client Assets: assets treated as client assets as specified in Part 7 of the Capital Market Institution Regulations.

Client Asset Rules: the rules relating to client assets contained in Part 7 of the Capital Market Institutions Regulations.

Client Money: money treated as client money as specified in Part 7 of the Capital Market Institutions Regulations.

Client Money Rules: the rules relating to client money contained in Part 7 of the Capital Market Institutions Regulations.

Close Links: in the Capital Market Institutions Regulations, the Credit Rating Agencies Regulations and the Securities Central Counterparties Regulations, means the relationship between a person (who is an applicant for authorization, a Capital Market Institution, an authorised credit rating agency or a CCP) and any of the following persons:

1. a controller of that person;

2. a company controlled by that person;

3. a company controlled by a controller of that person; or

4. a company controlled by any combination of the persons described in (1), (2) or (3) above.

Closed-Ended Investment Fund: any investment fund which is not an open-ended investment fund.

Closed-Ended Investment Traded Fund: a closed-ended investment fund, the units of which are traded on the Main Market or the Parallel Market.

Collateral: for the purposes of the Client Money Rules and Client Asset Rules, means money or an asset which has been paid for in full by a client and which is held by the Capital Market Institution or under its charge, either for its own account or under the terms of a deposit, pledge or other pledge arrangement.

Combating-Terrorism Crimes and its Financing Law: The Combating-Terrorism Crimes and its Financing Law issued by the Royal Decree No. M/21 dated 12/2/1439H.

Commercial Paper: a debt instrument creating or acknowledging indebtedness that has a maturity of less than one year from the date of issue.

Committee: the Committee for the Resolution of Securities Disputes established pursuant to paragraph (a) of Article 25 of the Capital Markets Law. Art. 1, Securities Disputes Proceedings Regulations; the Committee for the Resolution of Securities Disputes. Art. 1, Capital Markets Law

Commodities: food, metal, natural resources or other fixed physical substances in which contracts for future delivery are presently or in the future dealt in.Art.1(f), Prudential Rules

Companies Law: the Companies Law issued by Royal Decree No. (M/3) dated 28/1/1437H.

Competition Law: The Competition Law issued by Royal Decree No. M/75 dated 29/6/1440H.

Complaint and Suit: without prejudice to these term's meanings in the Capital Markets Law, each term shall, in relation to the application of these Regulations, bear the following meaning: Complaint: filing a claim (against decisions and actions taken by the authority or the exchange), a right's request or defending a right with the authority. Art. 1, Securities Disputes Proceedings Regulations, see "Suit."

Compliance Committee: the committee that is set up by a Capital Market Institution to monitor the securities business that it carries on.

Compliance Officer: the compliance officer of the Capital Market Institution appointed in accordance with paragraph (a) of Article 57 of the Capital Market Institutions Regulations, or the compliance officer of the external party delegated by the Capital Market Institution to function as a compliance officer, appointed in accordance with paragraph (e) of Article (20) of the Capital Market Institutions Regulations.

Conflict of Interest: Refers to the conflict of

interest between the issuer and any of the participating entities involved in the book building process, including but not limited to the following circumstances:

a) A director or an executive of any of the participating entities is a substantial shareholder in the issuer or any company that controls the issuer or any of the issuer's subsidiaries or vice versa.

b) A participating entity is a substantial shareholder in the issuer or any of the issuer's subsidiaries or vice versa.

c) Any of the persons, referred to in paragraph (a) and (b) above, is a director of the issuer or any of the issuer's subsidiaries. Art. 2(c), IPO Book Building

Connected Advisor: means in the Merger & Acquisition Regulations:

1) an advisor that is advising the offeror or the offeree company in relation to an acquisition (whether through a private transaction or an offer);

2) a Capital Market Institution acting for the benefit of the offeror or the offeree company; and

3) an advisor that is advising a person who is acting in concert with the offeror or the offeree company in relation to an offer or in relation to the matter which is the reason for that person being a member of the relevant concert party.

Connected Fund Manager: a fund manager of an investment fund who normally is connected with the offeror or the offeree company, as the case may be, if it is controlled by, controls or is under the same control as:

1) an offeror or any person acting in concert with it;

2) the offeree company or any person acting in concert with it; or

3) any connected advisor to any person above mentioned in (1) or (2).

Connected Person: the managing director, a director, the senior executives, any shareholder who owns a substantial percentage of shares of a company with a listed securities, or any associate of any such persons to whom this definition applies.

Constructionally Developed Real Estate: the real estates that are developed and ready for use and which fulfills the regulatory requirements, including residential, commercial, industrial, agricultural real estates and other types of real estates.

Contingent Liability Security: a derivative under the terms of which the client will or may be liable to make further payments when the instrument expires or the position is closed out.

Contingent Liability Transaction: a transaction in a contingent liability security.

Contract for Differences: any contract for differences or any other contracts the purpose or pretended purpose of which is to secure a profit or avoid a loss by reference to fluctuations in:

1) the value or price of property of any description; or

2) an index or other factor designated for that purpose in the contract;

but excluding:

1) rights under a contract if the parties intend

that the profit is to be secured or the loss avoided by one or more of the parties taking delivery of any property to which the contract relates;

2) rights under a contract under which money is received by way of deposit on terms that any return to be paid on the sum deposited will be calculated by reference to a specific index or other factor; and

3) rights under a contract of insurance.

Contractually Based Security: any of the following:

1) options;

2) futures;

3) contracts for differences;

4) long term insurance contracts;

5) any right to or interest in anything which is specified by any of the previous sub-paragraphs.

Control: the ability to influence the actions or decisions of another person through, whether directly or indirectly, alone or with a relative or affiliate (a) holding 30% or more of the voting rights in a company, or (b) having the right to appoint 30% or more of the members of the governing body; "controller" shall be construed accordingly.

Controlling Interest: The ability to influence actions or decisions of another person directly, indirectly, individually or collectively with a relative or an affiliate through: (A) owning 30% or more of the voting rights in a company, (B) having the right to appoint 30% or more of the administrative team members. Art.1, Regulatory Rules and Procedures issued pursuant to the Companies Law relating to Listed Joint Stock Companies. The ability to influence actions or decisions of another person directly, indirectly, individually or collectively with a relative or an affiliate through: (A) owning 30% or more of the voting rights in a company, (B) having the right to appoint 30% or more of the administrative team members. Art. 1, Corporate Governance Regulations

Convertible Currency: a currency that can be bought or sold without restrictions imposed by any governmental authority in the Kingdom or in the jurisdiction which has issued the currency. Article 2, Securities Central Counterparts Regulations

Counterparty: a client who is an Authorized Person, an exempt person, an institution or a non-Saudi financial services firm. Art.2, AML Regs. In the Capital Market Institutions Regulations and in the definition of the term "institutional client" stipulated in the Glossary, means any of the following:

1) SAMA;

2) The Exchange, or any other exchange recognized by the Authority;

3) The depository center;

4) The CCP;

5) A Capital Market Institution;

6) A Local Bank;

7) A local insurance company;

8) A qualified foreign investor; and

9) A non-Saudi financial services firm.

and otherwise, counterparty means a counterparty to a transaction.

Corporate Actions: actions taken by an issuer which lead to increasing or decreasing the number of its securities or changing its nominal value including, for example, increasing or decreasing its capital.

Corporate Finance Business: securities business carried on by a Capital Market Institution connection with:

1) the offer, issue, underwriting, repurchase, exchange or redemption of, or the variation of the terms of, those securities, or any related matter;

2) the manner in which, or the terms on which, or the persons by whom, any business activity is to be financed, structured, managed, controlled, regulated or reported upon;

3) an actual or proposed takeover or related operations; or

4) a merger, de-merger or reorganization.

Corporate Finance Professional: an employee of a Capital Market Institution who engages in corporate finance business.

Corporate Governance: rules to lead and guide the Company that includes mechanisms to regulate the various relationships between the Board, Executive Directors, shareholders and Stakeholders, by establishing rules and procedures to facilitate the decision making process and add transparency and credibility to it with the objective of protecting the rights of shareholders and Stakeholders and achieving fairness, competitiveness and transparency on the Exchange and the business environment.

Corporate Governance Regulations: Corporate Governance Regulations issued by the Board of the Authority.

Council of Competition Protection: the

Council of Competition Protection as constituted under the Competition Law.

Credit Rating: an opinion regarding the creditworthiness of an entity, or the creditworthiness of a security expressed in symbols, letters, numbers or any other form.

Credit Rating Agencies Regulations: the Credit Rating Agencies Regulations issued by the Board of the Capital Market Authority.

Credit Risks: risk of loss resulting from fluctuations in the credit standing of issuers of securities, counterparties and any debtors to which Authorized Persons are exposed. Art. 1(f), Prudential Rules. See, Market Risk

Cumulative voting: a method of voting for electing Board members that gives each shareholder a voting capacity equivalent to the number of shares he/she owns , and by which the shareholder is entitled to either exercise all of his/her votes towards one nominee or to divide his/her votes towards several nominees without any duplication of such votes. Art.1, Corporate Governance Regulations

Custodian: a person who is authorised under the Capital Market Institutions Regulations to conduct the securities activity of custody.

Custody: safeguarding assets belonging to another person which include securities, or arranging for another person to do so, and custody includes taking the necessary administrative measures.

Customer: in the Authorized Persons Regulations, means a client who is not a counterparty, whether it is an individual or a juristic person.

D

Day: a business day in the Kingdom in accordance with the official working days of the Authority. Under the Corporate Governance Regulations, "Day" means a calendar day whether a business day or not. Art. 1, Corporate Governance Regulations. Under the Securities Dispute Regulations, "Day" means: "the calendar day including official vacation days for the country. In relation to the dates mentioned in the Securities Dispute Regulations, if the last day is an official holiday then the date will be extended to the first business day thereafter." Art. 1, Securities Disputes Proceedings Regulations

Deal: to buy, sell, subscribe for or underwrite a security.

Dealing: to deal in a security, whether as principal or agent, and dealing includes the sale, purchase, manage the subscription or underwrite securities.

Dealing Day: any day on which the units of an investment fund may be subscribed for and redeemed.

Debt Instrument: tradeable instrument creating or acknowledging indebtedness issued by companies, the government, public institutions or public organizations, but excluding:

1) an instrument creating or acknowledging indebtedness for the consideration payable under a contract for the supply of goods or services, or for money borrowed to defray the consideration payable under a contract for the supply of goods or services;

2) a cheque, a bill of exchange, a banker's draft or a letter of credit;

3) a banknote, a statement showing a balance on a bank account, or a lease contract or any other evidence of disposition of property; and

4) a contract of insurance.

Debt-Based Recourse Debt Instrument: means a debt instrument issued by a special purposes entity under whose terms:

(a) the entitlement of holders of the debt instrument to a return is not based on the returns generated by the special purposes entity's assets;

(b) the sponsor is obliged to the holders of the debt instrument (whether by guarantee or otherwise) to pay all amounts due on the debt instrument; and

(c) repayment of the nominal value of the debt instrument is to be made to the holders of the debt instrument at or before the maturity of such debt instrument.

Demerged Entity: the entity that is the subject of a Demerger transaction resulting in it being spun-off, split-off or carved out from the Listed Company.

Demerger: a transaction where a Listed Company wishes to effect the separation or divesture of a subsidiary, an asset or a business wholly or partly within its existing group whether through a separate listing of such subsidiary, asset or business on the Exchange or without listing. A Demerger could take the form of a spin-off, a split-off or a carve out.

Depositary Bank: a financial institution of legal personality authorized to issue and cancel Depositary Receipts out of the Kingdom, appointed by the Issuer in accordance with the provisions of the Instructions on Issuing Depositary Receipts Out of the Kingdom. Art. 2(c), Instructions on Issuing Depositary Receipts out of the Kingdom

Depositary Receipts: Financial instruments listed and traded in a Foreign Market, issued by the Depositary Bank for shares issued in the Kingdom and listed in the Exchange, or for shares issued in the Kingdom and its Issuer has made the necessary arrangements for listing them in the Exchange. Art. 2(c), Instructions on Issuing Depositary Receipts Outside of the Kingdom

Derivative: a contract for differences, a future or an option. See, Contract for Differences.

Designated Securities: Securities in respect of which the CCP has issued a notice designating such Securities as not benefitting from the Clearing service. Article 2, Securities Central Counterparts Regulations

Developer: a person nominated by the fund manager to be responsible for executing the technical aspects to achieve the fund's purposes.

Direct Clearing Member: has the meaning specified in paragraph (a) of Article 21 of the Securities Central Counterparts Regulations. Article 2, Securities Central Counterparts Regulations.

Director: in relation to a joint stock company, includes a member of the board of directors and in relation to any other company includes any manager or other senior executive who makes and implements the company's strategic decisions.

Direct Financing Fund: An investment fund established for the purpose of carrying out the activity of direct financing for legal persons and investment funds. Art 2(d), Direct Financing Investment Funds Instructions.

Discretionary Account: means in the Merger and Acquisition Regulations, an account with a Capital Market Institution who is authorised to carry on managing activities, with the power to make investment decisions without prior reference to the holder of the account.

Distributor: for the purposes of the Investment Funds Regulations and the Real Estate Investment Funds Regulations, means; a person that is assigned to offer of units of an investment fund in the Kingdom.

Dual Unit Price: A settlement of the unit price calculated, in accordance with the financial statements, to which the expected credit losses are registered in the financial statements of the fund, against the unit price calculated for dealing purposes.

E

Edaa: the Securities Depository Centre Company
.

Employee: in relation to a person, includes a director or manager of a company, a partner in a partnership or any other individual who is employed under a contract of service or contract for service and whose services are placed at the disposal of and under the control of that person.

Employees' Shares: Treasury Shares which are allocated by the Company to its employees. Art.1, Regulatory Rules and Procedures issued pursuant to the Companies Law relating to Listed Joint Stock Companies.

Entities Subject to the Authority's Supervision (ESAS): for the purposes of these Rules, it shall mean the following:

1) The Exchange.

2) The Depositary Center.

3) Authorised persons licensed to carry on securities business, except authorised persons licensed to carry on arranging or advising activities.

4) Investment Funds.

5) Listed Companies. Art.2(c), Registration of Auditors.

Excess Exposures: large exposures in the trading book that exceed 25% of the Authorized Person's capital base. Art.1(f), Prudential Rules.

Exchange: the Saudi Stock Exchange Company ("Tadawul") or the Saudi Stock Exchange including where the context permits any committee, sub-committee, employee, officer, affiliate or agent to whom any function of the Exchange may for the time being be delegated, and "on Exchange" means any activity taking place through or by the facilities provided by the Exchange.

Exchange Rules: the regulations, rules, procedures and instructions proposed by the Board of Directors of the Exchange and approved by the Board of the Authority.

Exchange Traded Fund: an index fund that the units in which are traded on the Main Market or the Parallel Market.

Executive Director (of a company): a member of the Board who is a full time member of the executive management team of the Company and participates in its daily activities.

Execution-Only Customer: a customer for whom the authorised person only deals as agent in accordance with instructions provided by the customer and whom an authorised person does not advise.

Executive Board Member: means in the Capital Market Institutions Regulations, a member of the board of directors who is full-time in the executive management of the Capital Market Institution and participates in its daily activities.

Executive Management or **Senior Executive:** persons responsible for managing the daily operations of the Company, and proposing and executing strategic decisions, such as the Chief Executive Officer (CEO) and his/her delegates and the Chief Financial Officer (CFO). Art 1, Corporate Governance Regulations.

Exposures: items reported as assets in the balance sheet, derivatives reported as liabilities or off-balance sheet commitments.Art.1(f), Prudential Rules (see Excess Exposures, Large Exposures).

Exempt Offer: where:

a)

1) securities are issued by the government of the Kingdom;

2) offers of contractually based securities, provided that the offer of unlisted contractually based securities shall be limited to any of the following cases:

a. Where all offerees are investors under the categories of Institutional and Qualified Clients.

b. Where all offerees are employees of the issuer or of any of its affiliates.

3) where an issuer whose shares are not listed on the Exchange increases its capital by offering new shares to existing shareholders;

4) where the offeree is an affiliate of the issuer unless it is an offer of a class of shares that is listed on the Exchange;

5) where all of the offerees are employees of the issuer or of any of its affiliates unless it is an

offer of a class of shares that is listed on the Exchange; or

6) offers in an insolvency situation where shares are offered to creditors.

7) where an issuer whose shares are not listed on the Exchange increases its capital by way of debt conversion.

8) where the subscription in total value for the securities being offered is less than 10 million SR or an equivalent amount, in accordance to the following conditions:

a. The offer shall be not made more than one time during the twelve months after the completion of the offer.

b. Subscription in the offered securities shall be limited to (50) offerees or less (excluding investors under the categories of Institutional and Qualified Clients) provided that the amount payable per offeree (excluding investors under the categories of Institutional and Qualified Clients) shall not exceed (200,000) two hundred thousand SR or an equivalent amount.

c. Declaration by the offeree who participate in the subscription for such offered securities (excluding investors under the categories of Institutional and Qualified Clients) to the offeror or the Capital Market Institution (if the offer is carried out through a Capital Market Institution) of its acknowledgment to the risks associated with the investment, including what may result in loss of the full amount of the investment, and the that the Authority shall not give any assurance as to the accuracy and completeness of the documents related to the Offering or its completeness, and expressly disclaim any liability whatsoever for any loss arising from or incurred in reliance upon any part of these documents, and its acknowledgment that the offeror or the Capital Market Institution (if the offer is carried out through a Capital Market Institution) does not have to notify the Authority of the suitability of such an investment.

b) The offeror or the Capital Market Institution (if the offer is carried out through a Capital Market Institution) shall, when making an exempt offer, notify the Authority on a quarterly basis of the total number and value of the exempt offers the Capital Market Institution has made. In addition, the following information must be submitted to the Authority in respect of each exempt offer:

1) type of exempt offer;

2) categories of the offerees;

3) amount paid by each offeree category in Saudi riyals;

4) date of the commencement of the offering;

5) date of the completion of the offering;

6) name and nationality of the issuer;

7) name and nationality of the offeror;

8) price paid for each security;

9) type of security; and

10) total size of the offering.

11) Declaration by the offeree indicated in subparagraph (c) of paragraph (8) of this Article, including the following information:

a. The total amount payable per offeree who participate in the subscription for such securities and the number and description of the securities.

    b. Name of the offeree who participate in the subscription for such securities and its passport number or National ID and signature.

    c. Declaration date.

    c) The notification referred to in paragraph (b) of this Article must contain the information related to offers that are not complete as follows:

    1) on-going offerings;

    2) name of relevant issuer;

    3) name of relevant offeror;

    4) the expected date of completion of the offering; and

    5) type and class of the offered securities.

Exempt Person: any of the persons specified in Annex 1 to the Securities Business Regulations.

F

FATF: Financial Action Task Force on money laundering and terrorist financing. Art. 2, AML Regs.

Feeder Fund: an investment fund whose primary investment objective is to invest all of its assets in another investment fund.

Finance Company: a company licensed to engage in finance activities in accordance with the Laws of the Kingdom.

Financial Group: Comprises an Authorized Person and: 1) The Authorized Person's local and foreign subsidiaries that are regulated by these Rules or by similar rules; 2) Companies with which the Authorized Person has a joint, or essentially joint, management or exercises a significant influence over ; 3) Private equity investments in which the Authorized Person owns a majority of the voting rights. Art. 1(f), Prudential Rules

Financial Resources: in relation to a Capital Market Institution are the sum of the following:

1) shares other than cumulative preferences shares;

2) any sums standing to the credit of a share premium account;

3) audited reserves; and

4) revaluation reserves;

    less

1) intangible assets;

2) current year losses;

3) holdings of shares in other Capital Market Institutions, banks or non-Saudi financial service firms unless held for trading purposes only; and

4) illiquid assets.

Financial Sector Entities: any of the following:

1) banks;

2) capital market institutions;

3) legal persons engaged in the business of extending credit;

4) insurance companies;

5) finance companies;

6) affiliates of any of the above; or

7) any other entity which the Authority determines should be included or treated as a financial sector entity.

Financing Transaction: means the transaction under which a special purposes entity raises finance by the issue of debt instruments, including the acquisition, transfer or other use of assets required to generate amounts due under the terms of those debt instruments, and the issue of the debt instruments itself.

FIU: refers to the Financial Intelligence Unit of the Ministry of Interior. Art.2, AML Regs.

Fixed-term Subordinated Loans: the subordinated loans with a fixed term. These also include fixed term promissory notes. Art.I(f), Prudential Rules. See, "Subordinated Loans."

Foreign Credit Rating Agency: a credit rating agency incorporated in a jurisdiction other than the Kingdom and authorized or registered (as applicable) to conduct rating activities outside the Kingdom.

Foreign Fund: an investment fund, which is established in a jurisdiction outside the Kingdom.

Foreign Fund Manager: a person operating outside the Kingdom and working as a manager of a foreign fund.

Foreign Market: A regulated market for the trade of securities out of the Kingdom. Art. 2(c), Instructions on Issuing Depositary Receipts out of the Kingdom.

Foreign Portfolio Manager: a foreign financial institution that has a legal personality which manages the assets of clients, that meets the requirements stated in sub paragraph (a/2) of Article (6) of these Rules, which engages or intend to engage with the QFI or the applicant for the purpose of investing on its behalf in listed securities. Art. 2(c), Qualified Foreign Financial Institutions Regulations.

Foreign Regulator: in relation to a foreign credit rating agency, its principal regulator in the jurisdiction of its incorporation and/or establishment.

Foreign Strategic Investor: a foreign legal entity that aims to own a Strategic Shareholding in listed companies. Part 2(a), Foreign Strategic Ownership in Listed Companies

Freezing the Investment Account: The temporary block on all money transfers from the investment account, the utilization of its balance, and the transfer or pledge of securities in the investment portfolios linked to it. The freezing of the investment account shall not prevent the client from selling securities and receiving its proceeds or profits on the investment account or transferring funds from his bank account to his investment account. Art. 2(c), Investment Accounts Instructions.

Fundamental Change: means

1) a significant change in the fund's purposes, nature or class;

2) a change which may have a material adverse effect on the unitholders or their rights in relation to the closed-ended fund;

3) a change which alters the risk profile of the fund; or

4) the voluntary withdrawal of a Fund Manager from its position as the fund manager.

5) It usually causes unitholders to reconsider of their subscriptions in the closed-ended fund.

6) A change which results in any increased payments out of the assets of the closed-ended fund to a fund manager or any member of the fund board or an affiliate of either.

7) A change which introduces any new type of payment out of the assets of the closed-ended fund.

8) A change that materially increases other types of payment out of the assets of the closed-ended fund.

9) Change in the maturity date or termination of the closed-ended Fund.

10) Increase the total value of the ether fund assets by accepting cash or in-kind contributions, or both. Art.26(d), Real Estate Investment Funds Regulations.

Fund Board: the fund directors appointed by the fund manager in accordance with the Investment Funds Regulations and the Real Estate Investment Funds Regulations, to oversee and supervise the relevant fund manager's conduct.

Fund Director: a natural person appointed as a member of a fund board of an investment fund in accordance with the Investment Funds Regulations and the Real Estate Investment Funds Regulations.

Fund Management Fee: the remuneration, expenses and fees in relation to advisory services paid to the fund manager.

Fund Manager: the capital market institution that carries out the management of the assets of an investment fund or a real estate investment fund, and the management of its business and offering of its units in accordance with the Investment Funds Regulations, the Real Estate Investment Funds Regulations and the Rules for Special Purposes Entities.

Fund's Net Assets Value: for the purposes of the Investment Funds Regulations and the Real Estate Investment Funds Regulations, means; the Fund's Total Assets Value minus its liabilities.

Fund's Net Profit: for the purposes of the Real Estate Investment Funds Regulations, means the total revenues of the real estate investment fund after deducting the total expenses and fees incurred by the fund, except for the items of the other comprehensive income.

Fund of Funds: an investment fund the main objective of which is to invest all of its assets in other investment funds.

Fund Operator: the fund manager licensed to carry out the activity of managing investments and operating funds or the capital market institution appointed in accordance with paragraph (b) of Article 8 of the Investment Funds Regulations; to operate investment funds.

Fund Size: It means the Fund's Total Assets Value plus any capital pledged to be paid by the unitholders. Art. 2(d), Direct Financing Investment Funds Instructions.

Fund's Total Assets Value: for the purposes of the Investment Funds Regulations and the Real Estate Investment Funds Regulations it means; the fund's assets value that are valued based on the method of assets valuation stipulated in the Fund's Terms and Conditions.

Fund Sub-Custodian: A third party contracted by the custodian to perform some or all of the custodian's functions in relation to an investment fund.

Fund Sub-Manager: a third party contracted by a fund manager, under a contract, in accordance with the Investment Funds Regulations and the Real Estate Investment Funds Regulations, and takes on the fund manager's behalf all or part of the investment decisions for an investment fund managed by the fund manager.

Funds: means assets or properties of whatever type, material or intangible, movable or immovable, along with the legal documents and deeds proving the ownership of the assets or any right pertaining thereto. Art.2, AML Regs.

Future: rights under contracts for the sale of a commodity or property of any other description under which delivery is to be made at a prospective date and at a price agreed on when the contract is made, but excluding rights under any contract which is made for commercial and not investment purposes.

G

GCC: The Cooperation Council for the Arab States of the Gulf. Art. 2(c), Investment Accounts Instructions.

GCC Citizens: Natural persons who have the nationality of one of the GCC countries, and legal persons that the majority of their capital is owned by citizens of GCC countries or governments and has the nationality of one of the GCC countries. Art. 2(c), IPO Book Building.

GCC Companies: Companies that have the nationality of one of the GCC countries, and are incorporated according to the Companies Law of such country, and which the majority of their capital is owned by citizens of the GCC countries or their governments. Art. 2(c), IPO Book Building.

GCC Funds: The investment funds which have legal personality that are established in one of the GCC countries, the units of which are publicly or privately offered to investors in these countries according to the applicable laws in these countries, and which the majority of their capital is owned by citizens of the GCC countries or their governments. Art. 2(c), IPO Book Building.

GCC Legal Persons: A legal person whose capital is majority owned by citizens or governments of the GCC member states and holds the nationality of one of the GCC member states. Art. 2(c), Investment Accounts Instructions.

Geared Security: any of the following:

1) a contingent liability security; or

2) a vehicle which provides a return (or purports to provide a return) by gearing, whether by borrowing or by investing in contractually based securities.

General Assembly: the general assembly held with the attendance of the shareholders of the Company pursuant to the provisions of the Company's bylaws and the Companies Law. Art.1, Regulatory Rules and Procedures issued pursuant to the Companies Law relating to Listed Joint Stock Companies.

General Business Risk: the risks and potential losses arising from the CCP's operation as a business, but excluding risks and losses related to a Clearing Member default. General Business Risk includes any potential impairment of the CCP's financial position as a consequence of a decline in its revenues or an increase in its expenses. Article 2, Securities Central Counterparts Regulations.

General Clearing Member: has the meaning specified in paragraph (a) of Article 21 of the Securities Central Counterparts Regulations. Article 2, Securities Central Counterparts Regulations

Glossary: the Glossary of Defined Terms used in the Regulations and Rules of the Authority issued by the Board of the Authority.

Government Entities: Refers to any of the following: a) Entities which the Custodian of The Two Holy Mosques or the Council of Ministers are their point of reference for their financial and administrative affairs, including Ministries, Departments, Authorities, General Agencies, Government Funds or Funds managed by government entities. b) Legal persons affiliated to one of the GCC countries. Art. 2(c), IPO Book Building.

Government-owned Companies: Companies fully owned by the government or any government entity. Art. 2(c), IPO Book Building.

Government-related Entities: central banks, and investment funds -- including sovereign funds and funds which take the form of pension and endowments funds -- fully owned (directly or indirectly) by a government entity. Art. 2(c), Qualified Foreign Financial Institutions Regulations.

Group: in relation to a person, means that person and each affiliate of it. When referring to a person, means the person and his affiliates. Art.1, Corporate Governance Regulations.

Group of Connected Counterparties: two or more natural or legal persons who, unless otherwise shown, constitute a single risk because: 1) One of them, directly or indirectly, has control over the other or others in the group; or 2) they are so interconnected in a way that if one of them were to experience financial problems, the other or all of the others would be likely to encounter repayment difficulties. Art. 1(f), Prudential Rules.

Governing Body: the body of individuals which makes a person's strategic decisions, and the board of directors of a joint-stock company, or the board of managers of a limited liability company is considered its governing body.

H, I

Holding Company: a Joint Stock Company or Limited Liability Company aims to control other Joint Stock Companies or Limited Liability Companies called affiliates by owning more than half of those companies' share capitals or by controlling the composition of their management. Art. 1, Corporate Governance Regulations.

ICAAP: an acronym for "Internal Capital Adequacy Assessment Process," Prudential Rules, Chapter 20.

Identification Document: The valid identification document issued by the competent authorities and accepted for opening an investment account for the client in accordance with the Investment Accounts Instructions. Art. 2(c), Investment Accounts Instructions.

Illiquid Assets: means any of the following:

1) fixed assets;

2) financial resources which are not readily realisable; or

3) deposits not available for withdrawal within three months or less.

Implementing Regulations: any regulations, rules, instructions, procedures and orders issued by the Authority relating to the implementation of the Capital Market Law.

Independent Financial Advisor: means in the Merger & Acquisition Regulations, a financial advisor who is authorized by the Authority and is independent of its appointor (whether it is the offeror, offeree company or any other person obligated to appoint an independent financial advisor in accordance with the Merger & Acquisition Regulations). Circumstances under which the financial advisor shall not be considered independent of its appointor include, but are not limited to the following:

1) the financial advisor or any of its subsidiaries is a substantial shareholder in the appointor or any of its subsidiaries;

2) the financial advisor or any of its subsidiaries is a substantial shareholder in a controller of the appointer or any of its subsidiaries;

3) an employee of the financial advisor who is involved in the provision of financial advice to the person, is a substantial shareholder in the appointor or any of its subsidiaries;

4) any of the financial advisor's substantial shareholders or board member or in any of its subsidiaries is a substantial shareholders or board member with the appointer or in any of its subsidiaries;

5) any of the appointer's shareholders or board member or in any of its subsidiaries is a substantial shareholders or board member with the financial advisor or in any of its subsidiaries;

6) the appointor or any of its subsidiaries is a substantial shareholder in the financial advisor or any of its subsidiaries; or

7) the appointer or any of its subsidiaries is a substantial shareholder in a controller of the financial advisor or any of its subsidiaries.

Independent Fund Director: an independent fund director who enjoys complete independence by way of example, the following shall constitute an infringement of such independence:

1) he is an employee of the fund manager or any of its affiliates, or any sub-manager or custodian for a fund or have a material business, or contractual relationship with the fund manager or any sub-manager or custodian for such fund.

2) he, during the preceding two years, has been a senior executive of the fund manager or any of its affiliates.

3) he is a first-degree relative of any board member or any senior executives of the fund manager or of any its affiliates.

4) he is a controlling shareholder of the fund manager or any of its affiliates, during the preceding two years.

Independent Investment Advisor: the Capital Market Institution authorised to carry out advising business that holds itself out as an independent investment advisor in accordance with paragraph (f) of Article 41 of the Capital Market Institutions Regulations.

Independent Legal Advisor: means in the Merger & Acquisition Regulations, a legal advisor who is licensed to practice law in Saudi Arabia and is independent of its appointor (whether the offeror, offeree company or any other person obligated to appoint an independent legal advisor in accordance with the merger & acquisition regulations) and independent of the appointor's financial advisor. circumstances under which the legal advisor shall not be considered independent of its appointor include, but are not limited to the following:

1) the legal advisor or any of its subsidiaries is a substantial shareholder or board member in the appointor or in the financial advisor or any of their subsidiaries;

2) a partner of the legal advisor is a substantial shareholder or board member in a controller of the appointor or in the financial advisor or any of their subsidiaries;

3) an employee of the legal advisor, who is involved in the provision of legal advice and service to the person, is a substantial shareholder or board member in the appointor or in the financial advisor or any of their subsidiaries;

4) any partner or board member of the legal advisor or any of its subsidiaries is a substantial shareholder or board member in the appointor or in the financial advisor or any of their subsidiaries;

5) any of the appointer's substantial shareholders or board member or in any of its subsidiaries is a substantial shareholders or board member in the legal advisor or any of its subsidiaries;

6) the appointer of the legal or financial advisor or any of their subsidiaries is a substantial

shareholders or board member in the legal advisor or any of its subsidiaries; or

7) the appointer or any of its subsidiaries is a substantial shareholder in a controller of the legal advisor or any of its subsidiaries;

Independent Board Member: means in the Capital Market Institutions Regulations, a non-executive member of the board of directors who enjoys full independence in his position and decisions, and none of the negation of independence issues stipulated in paragraph (c) of Article 53 of the Capital Market Institutions Regulations, applies to him.

Independent Director: a non-executive member of the Board who enjoys complete independence in his/her position and decisions and none of the independence affecting issues stipulated in Article 20 of the Corporate Governance Regulations apply to him/her. Art. 1, Corporate Governance Regulations.

Independent Member: a non-executive member of the board who enjoys complete independence in his position and decisions, including having no business, family or other relationship that raises a conflict of interests regarding the CCP, its management or its Clearing Members, and who has had no such relationship during the five years preceding his membership of the board. Article 2, Securities Central Counterparts Regulations.

Index Fund: an investment fund whose primary investment objective is to track the performance of a specified index.

Initial Margin: margin that is collected to

cover the potential future exposure resulting from potential changes in the value of the Clearing Member's position over the appropriate close-out period in the event that Clearing Member defaults. Article 2, Securities Central Counterparts Regulations.

Inside Information: has the meaning specified at Article 4(c) of the Market Conduct Regulations: "inside information shall mean any security whose price or value would be materially affected if the information was disclosed or made available to the general public." Also see Art. 50, Capital Markets Law: "Insider information means information obtained by the insider and which is not available to the general public, has not been disclosed, and such information is of the type that a normal person would realize that in view of the nature and content of this information, its release and availability would have a material effect on the price or value of a Security related to such information, and the insider knows that such information is not generally available and that, if it were available, it would have a material effect on the price or value of such Security."

Insider: has the meaning specified at Article 4(b) of the Market Conduct Regulations.

Insolvency: actual insolvency, or the commencement of any proceedings in respect of insolvency, liquidation or a voluntary arrangement under the Bankruptcy Regulations, or the commencement of any equivalent procedures in the Kingdom or in any other jurisdiction outside the Kingdom.

Insolvent: a person to whom an insolvency event has occurred.

Inspection: Analyzing periodic data and information provided by the accounting firm and inspecting and assessing the quality control system and the degree of compliance with it. Art.2(c), Registration of Auditors

Institution:

1) any company which owns, or which is a member of a group which owns, net assets of not less than 10 million Saudi Riyals;

2) any unincorporated body, partnership or other organization which has net assets of not less than 10 million Saudi Riyals;

3) a person acting in the capacity of director, officer or employee of a legal person and responsible for its securities activity, where that legal person falls within the definition of paragraphs (1) or (2).

Institutional Client: means any of the following:

a. the Government of the Kingdom or any supranational authority recognized by the Authority.

b. companies fully owned by the government or any government entity, either directly or through a portfolio managed by a Capital Market Institution authorized to carry on managing business.

c. any legal person acting for its own account and be any of the following:

1) a company which owns, or is a member of a group which owns, net assets of more than 50 million Saudi Riyals;

2) an unincorporated body, partnership company or other organization which has net assets of more than 50 million Saudi riyals.

3) a person acting in the capacity of director, officer or employee of a legal person and responsible for its securities activity, where that legal person falls within the definition of paragraph (c/1) or (c/2).

d. a company fully owned by a legal person who meets the criteria of paragraph (b) or (c).

e. an investment fund.

f. a counterparty.

Instruction: any instruction, election, acceptance or any other message of any kind sent or received by way of the Tadawul Trading System or the Tadawul Depositary System.

Insurance Company: an insurance company which is regulated by SAMA. also, "a financial institution that has a legal personality which engages in insurance business." Art. 2(c), Qualified Foreign Financial Institutions Regulations

Intangible Assets: non cash assets, without physical substance, capable of providing the firm with services or benefits in the future, and in which the firm has acquired the right as a result of events that have occurred or operations that have been completed in the past. Intangible assets could be separately identifiable (could be separated from other assets), such as formation costs, trademarks, copyrights, industrial samples and designs, franchises and licenses. Intangible assets could also be unidentifiable in a separate manner such as goodwill, management skills and qualifications, and other factors which constitute the reputation.

Intermediate Broker: a person through whom a Capital Market Institution undertakes a margined transaction for a client.

Internal Regulations: the regulations issued by the Authority in relation to the Authority's administrative and financial affairs and its personnel and staff affairs. Art. 1, Capital Markets Law.

Interoperability Arrangement: an arrangement between two or more CCPs that involves a cross system execution of transactions. Article 2, Securities Central Counterparts Regulations.

Investment Account: An accounting record created by the authorized person for the client's money deposited in a client account opened by the authorized person to fund the client's transactions in securities and reflects all the details of the transactions in respect of that account.Art. 2(c), Investment Accounts Instructions.

Investment Advisor: an employee of a Capital Market Institution who performs the activity of advising on behalf of a Capital Market Institution with or for a client. an adviser who provides, offers or agrees to provide, advice to others in their capacity as investors or potential investors, in relation to purchasing, selling, subscribing or underwriting a security, or exercising any right conferred by a security to acquire, dispose of, underwrite or convert a security. Art. 1, Capital Markets Law.

Investment Fund: a collective investment scheme aimed at providing investors therein with an opportunity to participate collectively in the profits of the scheme which is managed by a fund manager for specified fees. Also, means any of the following legal persons:

1) a pension fund in which its main objective is to collect fees or periodic contributions from participants or for their interest, for the purpose of compensating them according to a specific mechanism.

2) Endowment fund with a principal purpose of making grants to organizations, institutions, or individuals for scientific, educational, cultural purposes, including university endowments fund.

3) a collective investment scheme aimed at providing investors therein with an opportunity to participate collectively in the profits of the scheme. Art. 2(c), Qualified Foreign Financial Institutions Regulations.

Investment Funds Regulations: the Investment Funds Regulations issued by the Board of the Authority.

Investment Grade: for the purposes of the Investment Funds Regulations, means; the rating category associated with relatively low default risks granted by recognized credit rating agencies.

Investment Portfolio: An account linked to the investment account that reflects the client's assets received by the authorized person in the course of carrying out securities business as per the Client Asset Rules stipulated in the Authorized Persons Regulations and reflects all the details of the transactions in respect of that account. Art. 2(c), Investment Accounts Instructions.

In Writing: or other similar term, wherever it

appears, in relation to a communication, notice, approval, agreement or other document, means in legible form and capable of being reproduced on paper, irrespective of the medium used.

Issuance Program: a program under which a single prospectus under the Rules on the Offer of Securities and Continuing Obligations is produced pursuant to which a number of debt instruments or convertible debt instruments may be issued in the future, as stated in the prospectus.

Issuer: a person issuing or intending to issue securities.

J, K

Joint Enterprise: an arrangement between two or more persons for commercial purposes related to a business which they carry on or are to carry on jointly.

Kingdom: the Kingdom of Saudi Arabia.

Large Exposures: an exposure to a counterparty or group of connected counterparties that exceeds 10% of the Authorized Person's capital base. Art.1(f), Prudential Rules

Lead Plaintiff: A person who represents Members of the Group of Plaintiffs in the proceedings before the Committees for the Resolution of Securities Disputes in connection with a Class Action Suit, and is appointed in accordance with the provisions of paragraph (b) of Article 56 of the Securities Disputes Regulations. Art. 1, Securities Disputes Proceedings Regulations.

Lead Rating Analyst: a rating analyst with primary responsibility for elaborating a credit rating or for communicating with the rated entity or the issuer of the security which is rated or to be rated.

Liability: any liability, loss, damage, claim or expense of any kind or nature, whether direct, indirect, consequential or otherwise.

Limited Offer: has the meaning specified in

Article 9 of the Rules on Offers of Securities and Continuing Obligations.

Limited Offer: An offer of securities is a limited offer if at the subscription is limited to no more than 100 offerees (excluding investors under the categories of Institutional and Qualified Clients) and the amount payable per offeree does not exceed 200,000 (two hundred thousand SR) or an equivalent amount. Limited to one such offer per 12 month period.

Liquidation of the Fund: means wherever mentioned in the Investment Funds Regulations and the Real Estate Investment Funds Regulations, a maximum period of 6 months from the next day of the date for the Termination of the Fund, during which the assets of fund must be fully liquidated in accordance with the provisions of the Investment Funds Regulations and the Real Estate Investment Funds Regulations.

Liquid Net Assets: assets funded by equity (common stock, disclosed reserves or other retained earnings) which are not otherwise encumbered and freely available to cover General Business Risk. Article 2, Securities Central Counterparts Regulations.

Listed: in relation to any type of securities, means the securities admitted to listing on the Exchange.

Listed Company: any company with securities of any kind listed on the Exchange.

Listing: listing securities on the Exchange either on the Main Market or on the Parallel Market, or, where the context permits, the application for listing.

Listing Rules: the Listing Rules proposed by the Board of the Exchange and approved by the Board of the Authority.

Local Bank: an institution that has received a license to engage in banking business in accordance with the Laws of the Kingdom.

Long Term Insurance Contract: any long term insurance contract specified by the Authority.

... Listing Rules: the Listing Rules proposed by
the Board of the Exchange and approved by the
board of the Authority.

Local Bank: an institution that has received a
license to engage in banking business in accordance with the Laws of the Kingdom.

Long Term Insurance Contract: any long
term insurance contract specified by the Authority.

M

Main Market: the market of exchange where securities, that have been registered and offered pursuant to Part 4 of the Rules on the Offer of Securities and Continuing Obligations, are traded.

Managing: managing securities belonging to another person in circumstances involving the exercise of discretion, or operating investment funds.

Managing Investments: making investment decisions for non-real estate investment funds and clients' portfolios in circumstances involving the exercise of discretion.

Managing Investments and Operating Funds: making investment decisions for investment funds and clients' portfolios in circumstances involving the exercise of discretion, and operating investment funds.

Margin: a Variation Margin or an Initial Margin. Article 2, Securities Central Counterparts Regulations

Margin Transaction: a transaction where a

Capital Market Institution makes a loan to a client of a portion of the cost of the transaction.

Market Conduct Regulations: the Market Conduct Regulations issued by the Board of the Capital Market Authority.

Market Maker: means in the Investment Funds Regulations, a capital market institution that is authorized to carry out dealing business where it enters continuous orders, during the trading hours, of buying and selling for the purpose of providing liquidity to the traded units of the exchange traded fund.

Market Risk: risk of loss resulting from fluctuations in the level and in the volatility of market prices of assets, liabilities and financial instruments. Art. 1(f), Prudential Rules. See, Credit Risks.

Member: a member of the committee appointed by its establishment resolution and any member added to the committee or appointed as a substitute of a former member. This term includes the committee's chairman unless the contrary intention appears. Art. 1, Securities Disputes Proceedings Regulations.

Members of the Group of Plaintiffs: A group of persons who participate in filing a Class Action Suit. Art. 1, Securities Disputes Proceedings Regulations.

Merger: a transaction, however its nature, involving an offeree company listed on the exchange and resulting in any of the following:

1) the absorption of that offeree company by another company listed on the exchange.

2) the absorption of that offeree company by a company that is not listed on the exchange.

3) the formation of a new legal entity by merging two companies or more (including the offeree company).

Merger and Acquisition Regulations: the Merger and Acquisition Regulations issued by the Board of the Capital Market Authority.

Minimum Authorization Requirements: means in the Credit Rating Agency Regulations, the authorization requirements specified in Article 8, Article 9 and Article 10 (as applicable in the Credit Rating Agencies Regulations).

MLRO: the Money Laundering and Terrorism Financing Reporting Officer of the Capital Market Institution, appointed in accordance with Article 64 of the Capital Market Institutions Regulations, or the Money Laundering and Terrorism Financing Reporting Officer of the external party delegated by the Capital Market Institution to function as a Money Laundering and Terrorism Financing Reporting Officer, appointed in accordance with paragraph (e) of Article (20) of the Capital Market Institutions Regulations.

Money Laundering: refers to committing or attempting to commit any act for the purpose of concealing or disguising the true origin of funds acquired by means contrary to Shari'ah or law, thus making the funds appear as if they had come from a legitimate source. Art.2, AML Regs.

Money Market Fund: an investment fund the sole objective of which is to invest in short-term securities and money market transactions in accordance with the Investment Funds Regulations.

Money Market Transactions: means short-term deposits and trade finance contracts.

N

Net Assets Value: for the purposes of the Investment Funds Regulations and the Real Estate Investment Funds Regulations, means; the Fund's Net Assets Value divided by the number of units outstanding.

Non-Executive Board Member: means in the Capital Market Institutions Regulations, a member of the board of directors who is not full-time managing the Capital Market Institution and does not participate in its daily activities.

Non-Executive Director: a member of the Board who is not a full-time member of the management team of the Company and does not participate in its daily activities. Art. 1, Corporate Governance Regulations.

Non-profit Organizations Entities: refers to a legal person who is an entity or an organization that primarily engages in raising/collecting donations and/or disbursing funds for nonprofit purposes. Art 2, AML Regs.; any legal entity licensed to engage in collecting, receiving, or paying money for charitable, religious, cultural, educational, social, or solidarity purposes or other charitable activities. Art. 2(c), Investment Accounts Instructions.

Non-Saudi Financial Services Firm: a person who engages in securities business in the course of his profession or trade outside the Kingdom.

Non-Trading Activities: the positions that are held for non-trading purposes. Art. 1(f), Prudential Rules.

Novation: a process whereby the original contract between one party and another party is discharged and replaced with two new contracts, one between the CCP and the first party and the other between the CCP and the second party. Article 2, Securities Central Counterparts Regulations.

O

Offer: means in the Merger & Acquisition Regulations, a general tender offer, other than the offers provided by the offeree company itself, that is subject to the Merger & Acquisition Regulations, made to all holders of the shares carrying voting rights in the offeree company for any of the following purposes:

1) purchase shares carrying Voting Rights in the offeree company or

2) to effect a merger of the offeree company.

Any reference in the Merger & Acquisition Regulations to the term "offer" or "potential offer" shall be construed as the following:

1) a merger or potential merger;

2) an offer or partial offer for takeover, or a potential offer or partial offer for takeover; or

3) partial offer or potential partial offer, not intended for takeover.

Offer Document: the offer document that the offeror is required to prepare and publish in relation to an offer, in accordance with Article 38 of the Merger & Acquisition Regulations.

Offeree Company: means in the Merger and Acquisition Regulations, a company listed on the Exchange (or unlisted company in the case of reversed takeover) in respect of which a takeover offer has been made.

Offering of Securities: See, Placement or Offering of Securities.

Offeror: means in the Rules on the Offer of Securities and Continuing Obligations, a person who makes an offer or invites a person to make an offer which, if accepted, would give rise to the issue or sale of securities by him or by another person with whom he has made arrangements for the issue or sale of the securities; and in the Merger and Acquisition Regulations, a person who makes or intends to make a takeover offer that is subject to the Merger and Acquisition Regulations.

Offeror: a person who makes or intends to make an Offer. The term also includes (where found in the Merger & Acquisition Regulations) any person(s) whom the offeror is acting in concert with. Moreover, "potential offeror" shall be construed accordingly.

Offer Period: the period from announcing a confirmed intention to provide an offer until the offer becomes unconditional as to acceptance, or until the extraordinary general assembly issues a decision to the offeror, as the case may be, and the offeree company in case of acquisition by an offer to exchange securities against the total shares of the offeree company.

Open-Ended Investment Fund: an invest-

an authority outside the Kingdom recognized by the Authority; or

3) an investment firm that is licensed to provide custody services and that is a member of a securities or futures exchange that is recognized by the Authority.

an authority outside the Kingdom recognized by the Authority; or

8) an investment firm that is licensed to provide custody services and that is a member of a securities or futures exchange that is recognized by the Authority.

P

Parallel Market: the market of Exchange where shares, that have been registered and offered pursuant to Part 8 of the Rules on the Offer of Securities and Continuing Obligations, are traded.

Partial Offer: an offer (except for offers made by the same offeree company) subject to the Merger & Acquisition Regulations, made to all holders of the shares carrying voting rights in the offeree company to purchase a certain percentage of shares in the offeree company.

Participating Entities: Entities involved in the Book building process from the specified parties in Part (5) of the IPO Book Building Instructions.Art. 2(c), IPO Book Building.

Participating Parties: Those whom are entitled to participate in the Book building process as specified in Part (5) of the IPO Book Building Instructions. Art. 2(c), IPO Book Building.

Pass-Through Service: a service offered by the CCP in respect of Designated Securities to facilitate their settlement without providing

Clearing services. Article 2, Securities Central Counterparts Regulations.

Percentage Ratio: in relation to a transaction, the figure, expressed as a percentage, that results from applying a calculation under a Class Test to the transaction.

Permitted Business Profile: the authorized business profile of a Capital Market Institution.

Perpetual Subordinated Loans: the subordinated loans with no fixed term.Art. 1(f), Prudential Rules. See, "Subordinated Loans."

Person: any natural or legal person recognized as such under the laws of the Kingdom.

Placement or Offering of Securities: issuing securities, inviting the public to subscribe therefor or the direct or indirect marketing thereof; or any statement, announcement or communication that has the effect of selling, issuing or offering securities, but does not include preliminary negotiations or contracts entered into with or among underwriters. Art. 1, Capital Markets Law.

Pledge: any form of a security interest recognized under the laws of the Kingdom capable of taking effect in relation to a security.

Politically Exposed Person (PEP): is any individual who occupies, has recently occupied, is actively seeking or is being considered for, a senior civil position in a government of a country, state or municipality or any department including the military, any agency, government-owned company. The definition of PEP includes members of immediate family and close associates, collectively known as Related Individuals. Immediate family is typically defined as any known individual who is a member of the PEP's immediate family (i.e. spouse, parent, sibling or child). Close associate is defined as any individual who is a senior advisor closely associated with or an agent of the PEP.

PEP (Amendment): Politically Exposed Persons (PEPs)PEPs refers to any of the following categories: Individuals who are or have been entrusted with prominent public functions domestically or in a foreign country, for example Heads of State or of government, senior politicians, senior government, judicial or military officials, senior executives of state owned corporations, and important political party officials. Persons who are or have been entrusted with a prominent function by a regional or international organization as members of senior management, including directors, deputy directors and members of the board or equivalent functions. The PEPs definition covers the family members or relatives of the individuals, and does not cover the middle ranking or more junior individuals in the foregoing categories." (Amendment issued 02/10/2017)

Portfolio Manager: an employee of a Capital Market Institution who performs the activity of managing on behalf of a Capital Market Institution with or for a client.

Position: the Authorized Person's own market position and market position that derive from its activities on behalf of clients or as a market maker.Art. 1(f), Prudential Rules.

Positions Held With Trading Intent: the positions that are held intentionally for short-term resale and/or with the intent of benefiting from actual or expected short-term price movements or to lock in arbitrage profits. Art. 1(f), Prudential Rules.

Prepared Securities Advertisements: has the meaning given to it in the Capital Market Institutions Regulations.

Price Stabilization Mechanism: A mechanism that contribute to the price stabilization of the newly listed shares on the Exchange, by means of over-allotment, and where all or any of the following transactions are conducted:

a) Borrowing a number of shares from lending-shareholders prior to the initial public offering, in an amount not exceeding the number resulted from the maximum limit allowed for over-allotment.

b) The short selling of shares during the offer period.

c) The over-allotment of shares not exceeding the limit set out in paragraph (a) of Part 3 of these Instructions.

d) Purchasing of shares from the Exchange during the Price Stabilization Period or by a Purchase Option in order to close any position under paragraph (a) above. Part 2, IPO Price Stabilization Mechanism .

Price Stabilization Period: A period of time for the Price Stabilization Mechanism that is agreed upon between the price stabilization manager and the issuer, provided that such period shall not exceed (30) calendar days from the first day of listing the shares on the Exchange. Part 2, IPO Price Stabilization Mechanism.

Pricing Supplement: a document which contains the final terms of each debt instruments or convertible debt instruments issue which is intended to be listed.

Principles: the principles specified in Part 2 of the Capital Market Institutions Regulations.

Principles for Financial Market Infrastructures: the international standards for financial market infrastructures issued by the Committee on Payment and Market Infrastructures (CPMI) and the Technical Committee of the International Organization of Securities Commissions (IOSCO). Article 2, Securities Central Counterparts Regulations.

Private Fund: an investment fund which is established in the Kingdom and which is not a public fund, and the units in which may be offered by the fund manager, in accordance with Part Five of the Investment Funds Regulations, to investors in the Kingdom.

Private Placement: An offer of securities is a private placement where it is not an exempt offer, public offer or a Parallel Market Offer and falls under any of the following cases:

1) the subscription is restricted to investors under the categories of Institutional and Qualified clients; or

2) the offer is a limited offer. Offers of Securities Regulations, see also "Exempt Offer."

Private Placement: for the purpose of the Rules on the Offer of Securities and Continuing Obligations, means an offer of securities which falls within one of the categories of offers listed in Article 8 of the Rules on the Offer of Securities and Continuing Obligations; and for the purposes of the Investment Funds Regulations, means:

1) for private funds, the offer of units in accordance with paragraph (a) of Article 80 of the Investment Funds Regulations; and

2) for foreign funds, the offer of securities in accordance with paragraph (a) of Article 98 of the Investment Funds Regulations.

Private Placement Notification: the notification required to be made to the Authority under sub-paragraph (2) of paragraph (a) of Article 10 of the Rules on the Offer of Securities and Continuing Obligations. For the purposes of the Investment funds regulations, means the notification required to be made to the Authority under sub- paragraphs (1,2 and 3) of paragraph (a) of Article 81 of the Investment Funds Regulations in relation to private funds or under sub-paragraphs (1,2 and 3) of paragraph (a) of Article 99 of the Investment Funds Regulation in relation to foreign funds.

Private Real Estate Fund: a private fund the objective of which is to invest in real estate, and it does not include funds that invest all of its assets outside the Kingdom.

Private Transaction: transaction involving the purchase and/or sale of shares carrying Voting Rights in any company listed on the Exchange, negotiated between the Offeror and selling shareholder(s) of the Offeree Company without making an Offer or involving the other shareholders or directors of the Offeree Company.

Procyclical: the changes in risk-management requirements or practices that are positively correlated with business or credit cycle fluctuations and that may cause or exacerbate financial instability. Article 2, Securities Central Counterparts Regulations.

Professional Investor: any natural person who fulfills at least one of the following criteria:

1) has carried out at least 10 transactions per quarter over the last 12 months of a minimum total amount of 40 million Saudi Riyals on securities markets;

2) his net assets is not less than 5 million Saudi Riyals;

3) works or has worked for at least three years in the financial sector in a professional position which requires knowledge of securities investment;

4) holds professional certificate that is related to securities business and accredited by an internationally recognized entity; or

5) holds the General Securities Qualification Certificate that is recognized by the Authority, and has an annual income that is not less than 600,000 Saudi Riyals in the two most recent years.

Professional Standards: Accounting and auditing standards, the professional code of ethics and other standards and pronouncements adopted by the Saudi Organization for Certified Public Accountants. Art.2(c), Registration of Auditors.

Prospectus: the document required to offer securities in the Main Market or in the Parallel Market in accordance with the Capital Market Law and the Rules on the Offer of Securities and Continuing Obligations.

Public: means in the Rules on the Offer of Securities and Continuing Obligations, the Instructions on the Price Stabilization Mechanism In Initial Public Offerings and the Instructions on Issuing Depositary Receipts Out of the Kingdom, persons other than the following:

1) affiliates of the issuer;

2) substantial shareholders of the issuer;

3) directors and senior executives of the issuer;

4) directors and senior executives of affiliates of the issuer;

5) directors and senior executives of substantial shareholders of the issuer;

6) any relative of persons described at (1), (2), (3), (4) or (5) above;

7) any company controlled by any persons described at (1), (2), (3), (4), (5) or (6) above; or

8) persons acting in concert, with a collective shareholding of (5%) or more of the class of shares to be listed. For purposes of the Regulatory Rules and Procedures issued pursuant to the Companies Law relating to Listed Joint Stock Companies, the shares retained by the Company do not count as a part of the ownership of the public. Art.1, Regulatory Rules and Procedures issued pursuant to the Companies Law relating to Listed Joint Stock Companies.

Public Consultation: A request for public comments on an implementing regulations project. Art. 2(c), Public Consultations on Implementing Regulations.

Public Fund: an investment fund which is established in the Kingdom and the units in which may be offered by the fund manager, in accordance with Part Four of the Investment Funds Regulations, to investors in the Kingdom otherwise than by way of a private placement.

Public Unitholders: means in the Investment Funds Regulations and the Real Estate Investment Funds Regulations, any unitholder who own a unit or units in the closed-ended investment traded fund or the real estate investment traded fund other than the following:

1) Substantial Unitholder;

2) the fund manager and its affiliates; or

3) the fund's board of directors' members.

Purchase Option: A contractual option whereby the price stabilization manager is granted the right to buy an amount of shares not exceeding the amount of the shares included in the over-allotment at the subscription price in the initial offer period, during the price stabilization period or after its end. Part 2, IPO Price Stabilization Mechanism.

Purchased Shares: shares bought back by the Company pursuant to Article 112 of the Companies Law. Art.1, Regulatory Rules and Procedures issued pursuant to the Companies Law relating to Listed Joint Stock Companies.

Q

QFI: Qualified Foreign Investor. A QFI is a Qualified foreign investor to invest in securities listed in the Saudi Stock Exchange, in accordance with the Rules. Part A.1, Qualified Foreign Institutions FAQs.

Quality Control System: Policies and procedures approved by the accounting firm in order to reasonably verify the compliance of the firm's employees with the professional standards and related laws governing their performance in carrying on audit engagement, including the professional code of ethics approved by the Saudi Organization for Certified Public Accountants. Art.2(c), Registration of Auditors.

Qualified Foreign Investor: a qualified foreign investor in accordance with these Rules to invest in listed securities. Art. 2(c), Qualified Foreign Financial Institutions Regulations

QFI Assessment Agreement: an agreement between the Assessing Authorized Person and the QFI meeting the requirements set out in Article (10) of the Qualified Foreign Financial Institutions Regulations. Art. 2(c), Qualified Foreign Financial Institutions Regulations.

Qualified Client: means any of the following:

A) a natural person who meets at least one of the following criteria:

1) has carried out at least 10 transactions per quarter over the last 12 months of a minimum total amount of 40 million Saudi Riyals on securities markets;

2) his net assets is not less than 5 million Saudi Riyals.

3) Works or has worked for at least three years in the financial sector in a professional position related to investment in securities.

4) holds a professional certificate in securities business and accredited by an internationally recognized entity.

5) holds the General Securities Qualification Certificate that is recognised by the Authority, and has an annual income that is not less than 600,000 Saudi Riyals in the last two years.

6) being a client of a Capital Market Institution authorized by the Authority to conduct managing activities, provided that the following is fulfilled: a. the offer shall be made to the Capital Market Institution, and that all related communications be made by it. b. the Capital Market Institution has been appointed on terms which enable it to make investment decisions on the client's behalf without obtaining prior approval from the client.

7) registered persons of a Capital Market Institution if the offer is carried out by the Capital Market Institution itself.

B) a legal person, which meets at least one of the following criteria:

1) any legal person acting for its own account and be any of the following:

a. a company which owns, or which is a member of a group which owns, net assets of not less than 10 million Saudi Riyals and not more than 50 million Saudi Riyals.

b. any unincorporated body, partnership company or other organization which has net assets of not less than 10 million Saudi Riyals and not more than 50 million Saudi riyals.

c. a person acting in the capacity of director, officer or employee of a legal person and responsible for its securities activity, where that legal person falls within the definition of paragraph (1/a) or (1/b).

2) clients of a Capital Market Institution authorized by the Authority to conduct managing activities, provided that the following is fulfilled:

a. the offer shall be made to the Capital Market Institution, and that all related communications be made by it; and

b. the Capital Market Institution has been appointed on terms which enable it to make investment decisions on the client's behalf without obtaining prior approval from the client.

C) a company fully owned by a natural person who meets one of the criteria mentioned in paragraph (A) or a legal person who meets one of the criteria mentioned in paragraph (B).

Qualified Investor: means in Part 8 of the Rules on the Offer of Securities and Continuing Obligations, Articles 46 and 47 of the Investment

Funds Regulations and Article 45 of the Real Estate Investment Funds Regulations, any of the following:

1) Capital Market Institutions acting for their own account.

2) Clients of a Capital Market Institution by the Authority to conduct managing activities provided that this Capital Market Institution has been appointed as an investment manager on terms which enable it to make decisions concerning the acceptance of an offer and investment in the Parallel Market on the client's behalf without obtaining prior approval from the client.

3) The Government of the Kingdom, any government body, any supranational authority recognized by the Authority or the Exchange, and any other stock exchange recognized by the Authority or the Securities Depository Center.

4) Government-owned companies, either directly or through a portfolio managed by a Capital Market Institution authorized to carry out managing activities.

5) Companies and funds established in a member state of the Cooperation Council for the Arab States of the Gulf.

6) Investment Funds.

7) Non-resident foreigners permitted to invest in the parallel market and who meet the requirements stipulated in the Guidance Note for the Investment of Non-Resident Foreigners in the Parallel Market.

8) Qualified foreign financial institutions.

9) Any other legal persons allowed to open an

investment account in the Kingdom and an account at the Depositary Center.

10) Natural persons allowed to open an investment account in the Kingdom and an account at the Depositary Center, and fulfill any of the following criteria:

       a. Has conducted transactions in security markets of not less than 40 million Saudi riyals in total, and not less than ten transactions in each quarter during the last twelve months

       b. His net assets is not less than 5 million Saudi Riyals.

       c. works or has worked for at least three years in the financial sector.

       d. Holds the General Securities Qualification Certificate which is recognized by the Authority.

       e. holds a professional certificate that is related to securities business and accredited by an internationally recognized entity.

11) Any other persons prescribed by the Authority.

Qualifying Central Counterparty: a CCP that has demonstrated that it is established and operating consistently with the Principles for Financial Market Infrastructures. Article 2, Securities Central Counterparts Regulations.

R

Rated Entity: a legal person whose creditworthiness is explicitly or implicitly rated in the credit rating (including the issuer of the security to be rated), whether or not it has solicited that credit rating and whether or not it has provided information for that credit rating.

Rating Activities: any of the following activities: data and information analysis with a view to a credit rating; and the evaluation and approval and issue and review of a credit rating.

Ratio of Shares to Depositary Receipts: The number of Depositary Receipts for each of the Issuer's issued shares in the Kingdom. Art. 2(c), Instructions on Issuing Depositary Receipts Outside of the Kingdom.

Rating Analyst: a person who performs analytical functions in connection with rating activities.

Rating Category: a rating symbol, such as a letter or numerical symbol which might be accompanied by appending identifying characters, used in a credit rating to provide a relative measure of risk to distinguish the different risk characteristics of the types of rated entities, securities or other assets.

Ratio of Fund Costs to the Fund's Total Assets Value: the ratio of total fund costs to the most recent Fund's Total Assets Value during the relevant half or quarter. Fund costs shall mean; all the expenses incurred by the fund, including fixed and variable expenses, beside the expenses associated with specific events.

Real Estate Investment Fund: a collective real estate investment scheme aimed at providing investors therein with an opportunity to participate collectively in the profits of the scheme which is managed by a fund manager for specified fees.

Real Estate Investment Traded Fund (REIT): a real estate investment fund, the units of which are traded on the Main Market or the Parallel Market, and whose primary investment objective is to invest in constructionally developed real estates, able to generate periodic and rental income, and distribute a specified percentage of the fund's net profit in cash to the unitholders in such fund during its operation period, at least annually.

Real Estate Investment Funds Regulation: the Real Estate Investment Funds Regulation issued by the Board of the Authority.

Registration: Registration of the accounting firm or the CPA to carry on audit engagements for ESAS in accordance with the provisions of the Registration of Auditors Rules. Art.2(c), Registration of Auditors

Reconciliation: the identification and explanation of individual items of difference between two sets of records, but does not include the processing of necessary adjustments.

Registered Person: a person who is registered with the Authority to perform a registrable function.

Registered Shareholders: the shareholders registered in the Shareholders Register at the end of the day on which the Extraordinary General Assembly's meeting is held to approve the increase of the Company's share capital and issuance of related new shares or at the end of the day specified by the ordinary General Assembly or by the Board on which shareholders become entitled to dividends as to dividends distribution.Art.1, Regulatory Rules and Procedures issued pursuant to the Companies Law relating to Listed Joint Stock Companies

Registrable Functions: any of the functions that the Authority specifies must be performed by a person registered with the Authority.

Registration Document: the document required for the registration of shares with the Authority for direct listing on the Parallel Market pursuant to the Rules on the Offer of Securities and Continuing Obligations.

Regulatory Authority: the Authority, SAMA or any other authority in the Kingdom or overseas which regulates or supervises the conduct of securities, banking, financial, insurance or investment business including any self-regulating organization.

Regulatory Information Service Provider: means the Exchange or an alternative communication channel or platform recognized by the Authority that replaces the Exchange in cases when it's not possible for persons to make public announcements through the exchange.

Related Parties: mean, in the Investment Funds Regulations and the Real Estate Investment Funds Regulations, the following:

1) Fund manager and fund sub-manager.

2) Custodian and sub-custodian.

3) The developer and engineering office.

4) The property manager (where applicable).

5) The accredited valuer.

6) The auditor.

7) fund's board of directors.

8) Members of the board of directors, any of the executive managers or any employees of one of the above mentioned parties.

9) Any unitholder who owns more than (5%) of the fund's net assets.

10) Any person who controls or who is an affiliate of any of the above mentioned parties.

Related Parties: for the purposes of the Corporate Governance Regulations means:

A. Substantial Shareholders of the company.

B. Board members of the Company or any of its affiliates and their relatives.

C. Senior Executives of the Company or any of its affiliates and their relatives.

D. Board members and Senior Executives of Substantial Shareholders of the company.

E. Entities, other than companies, owned by a Board member or any Senior Executive or their relatives.

F. Companies in which a Board member or a

Senior Executive or any of their relatives is a partner.

G. Companies in which a Board member or a Senior Executive or any of their relatives is a member of its Board of directors or is one of its Senior Executives.

H. Joint stock companies in which a member of the Board or a Senior Executive or any of their relatives owns (5%) or more, subject to the provisions of paragraph (D) of this definition.

I. Companies in which a Board member or a Senior Executive or any of their relatives has influence on their decisions even if only by giving advice or guidance.

J. Any person whose advice or guidance influence the decisions of the Company, the Board and the Senior Executives.

K. Holding companies or affiliates. Art.1, Corporate Governance Regulations, but advice or guidance that is provided on a professional basis by a person licensed to provide such advice shall be excluded from the provisions of paragraphs (I) and (J) of this definition.

Related Party: in the Rules on the Offer of Securities and Continuing Obligations, means:

1) affiliates of the issuer;

2) substantial shareholders of the issuer;

3) directors and senior executives of the issuer;

4) directors and senior executives of affiliates of the issuer;

5) directors and senior executives of substantial shareholders of the issuer;

6) any relatives of persons described at (1), (2), (3), (4) or (5) above;

7) any company controlled by any person described at (1), (2), (3), (4), (5) or (6) above.

Related Party: In the Merger and Acquisition Regulations, means a person who, in relation to each of the offeror (or any of its affiliates) and the offeree company (or any of its affiliates), satisfies one or more of the following conditions:

1) any person who has provided financial assistance (other than a bank in the ordinary course of business) to the offeror or the offeree company;

2) the board members of the offeror or the offeree company (or any of their subsidiaries);

3) a person owning 20% of the offeror and the offeree (weather individually or by acting in concert with other(s))

4) a substantial shareholder with the offeror who in the same time is a board member in offeree company, or vice versa.

Relative: means in the Capital Market Institutions Regulations, parents, husband, wife, and children.

Relative: husband, wife and minor children.

Relative: means in the Merger and Acquisition Regulations, husband, wife, children and parents.

Relatives:

- Fathers, mothers, grandfathers and grandmothers (and their ancestors).
- children and grandchildren and their descendants.
- siblings, maternal and paternal half-siblings.
- Husbands and wives. Art. 1, Corporate

Governance Regulations; and "includes the husband, wife, children and parents."Art. 2(c), Reporting of Violations of Capital Market Law

Remuneration (and Compensation): means in the Capital Market Institutions Regulations, amounts, allowances, profits and the like, periodic or annual bonuses linked to performance, long or short-term incentive plans and any other in-kind benefits, except for the actual reasonable expenses and fees incurred by the company to enable a board member to perform his duties.

In the Capital Governance Regulations, means: amounts, allowances, dividends and the like, periodic or annual bonuses linked to performance, long or short term incentive plans and any other in-kind benefits except the actual reasonable expenses and fees incurred by the company to enable the Board member to perform his duties. Art. 1, Corporate Governance Regulations.

Also, "amounts, allowances, profits and their equivalent, periodic and annual performance-related bonuses, short and long term incentive plans, in addition to any other in-kind benefits, except for reasonable costs and expenses actually incurred by the Company on behalf of a Board member in performing his work." Art.1, Regulatory Rules and Procedures issued pursuant to the Companies Law relating to Listed Joint Stock Companies

Remuneration Committee: a committee formed pursuant to the provisions of the Corporate Governance Regulations. Art.1, Regulatory

Rules and Procedures issued pursuant to the Companies Law relating to Listed Joint Stock Companies

Report: means information provided to the Authority – through channels to be determined by the Authority – in relation to any acts or practices that constitute a violation of any provisions of the Law or its implementing regulations, or of the regulations of the Exchange, the Depository Center, or the Clearing Center.Art. 2(c), Reporting of Violations of Capital Market Law

Reported Individual: means a person against whom a report to the Authority was made in relation to any acts or practices that constitute a violation of any provisions of the Law or its implementing regulations, or of the regulations of the Exchange, the Depository Center, or the Clearing Center.Art. 2(c), Reporting of Violations of Capital Market Law

Reporting Individual: means a person who reports to the Authority any acts or practices that constitute a violation of any provisions of the Law or its implementing regulations, or of the regulations of the Exchange, the Depository Center, or the Clearing Center. Art. 2(c), Reporting of Violations of Capital Market Law

Restructuring: a material merger or reorganization, including a material restructuring as described in paragraph (6) of Article 23 of the Rules on the Offer of Securities and Continuing Obligations.

Retail Client: Any client who is not a qualified client or an institutional client.

Revaluation Reserve: a reserve account considered as a part of an Authorized Person's Tier-2 capital, that records the surplus created when a revaluation finds that the current value of an asset is higher than its recorded historical cost. The revaluation surplus may be reduced where a subsequent revaluation finds that the current value of an asset has decreased. Art. 1(f), Prudential Rules

Reverse Takeover: an arrangement where a listed company makes an offer of new shares in itself to the shareholders of an unlisted company in exchange for their shares and theses new shares will represent more than 50% of the listed company voting shares after the acquisition.

Reward: means a monetary amount determined based on the amount of the fines and financial penalties collected as a result of the Report.Art. 2(c), Reporting of Violations of Capital Market Law

Risk-Weight: a percentage that describes a risk level of an exposure under the non-trading activities. Art. 1(f), Prudential Rules

Rights Issue: an offer of additional shares to existing shareholders which enables those shareholders to subscribe in proportion to their existing holdings.

Rules for Special Purposes Entities: the Rules for Special Purposes Entities issued by the Board of the Authority.

Rules on the Offer of Securities and Continuing Obligations: the Rules on the Offer of Securities and Continuing Obligations issued by the Board of the Authority.

Sales Professional: an employee of a capital market institution who performs the activities of dealing or arranging on behalf of a capital market institution with or for a client.

SAMA: the Saudi Central Bank.

SBL (Securities Borrowing and Lending) Transaction: a privately negotiated trade settled in Depository Center accounts. (Securities Borrowing and Lending Regulations, Art. 2)

Securities: means any of the following:

1. shares;

2. debt instruments;

3. warrants;

4. certificates;

5. units;

6. options;

7. futures;

8. contracts for differences;

9. long term insurance contracts; and

10. any right to or interest in anything which is specified by any of the paragraphs (1) through (9) above.

balance sheet.Art. 1, Procedures for Listed Companies with Losses

Short-Selling Transactions: A short selling transaction means any sale of a borrowed listed security in accordance with the Securities Business Law Regulations.Art.3, Short Selling Regulations

Sophisticated Investor: for the purposes of the Rules on the Offer of Securities and Continuing Obligations, has the meaning specified in Article 9 of the Rules on the Offer of Securities and Continuing Obligations issued pursuant to the Authority's Board Resolution no. (3-123-2017) dated 09/04/1439 H. corresponding to 27/12/2017 G. and amended by the Authority's Board Resolution no. (1-104-2019) dated 01/02/1441 H. corresponding to 30/09/2019 G.; and for the purposes of the Investment Funds Regulations and the Capital Market Institutions Regulations, has the meaning specified in paragraph (b) of Article 74 of the Investment Funds Regulations issued pursuant to the Authority's Board Resolution No. (1-219-2006) dated 03/12/1427 H. corresponding to 24/12/2006 G. and amended by the Authority's Board Resolution No. (1-61-2016) dated 16/08/1437H. corresponding to 23/05/2016 G.

Special Assembly: the special assembly held with the attendance of holders of preferred shares of the same class in accordance with the Companies law, Company's bylaws and these rules and procedures.Art.1, Regulatory Rules and Procedures issued pursuant to the Companies Law relating to Listed Joint Stock Companies

Special Fund Resolution: means a resolution

requiring an affirmative vote of the unitholders of 75% or more of the units in the investment fund present or represented by proxy at a meeting of unitholders or by modern means of technology.

Special Purposes Entity: means an entity established and licensed under the Rules for Special Purposes Entities.

Specialized Public Fund: has the meaning specified in Article 53 of the Investment Funds Regulations.

Spin-Off: a type of Demerger where all or a portion of the shares in the spun-off entity/new entity to be formed to hold the asset, are distributed on a pro-rata basis to the Listed Company's shareholders as dividend, resulting in a full separation of the two entities in a single transaction. In a Spin-Off transaction a portion of the shares of the spun-off entity/new entity to be formed to hold the asset, may be offered to the public through a public offering and listing on the Exchange.

Split-Off: a type of Demerger transaction where the Listed Company makes an offer to its shareholders to exchange their parent shares which will be acquired by the Listed Company as treasury shares, in exchange for all or a portion of the shares of the spun-off entity/ new entity to be formed to hold the asset.

Sponsor: The person responsible for sponsoring the special purposes entity in accordance with the provisions of the Rules for Special Purposes Entities.

Stakeholder: any person who has an interest in the Company, including employees, creditors, customers, suppliers and the community. Art. 1, Corporate Governance Regulations.

Strategic Shareholding: the direct ownership percentage in the listed company's shares, and through which the aim is to contribute in promoting the financial or operational performance of the listed company.Part 2(a), Foreign Strategic Ownership in Listed Companies

Stress Testing: For the purposes of the Investment Funds Regulations it means, preparing stress tests models and methods for analyzing hypothetical cases of the risks facing the fund, and the fund manager's policy to address them. In addition to analyzing the level of sensitivity to measure the level of fluctuation in the prices of investment funds units for the variables that affect them. Including, but not limited to, the fund manager carrying out a hypothetical simulation of the liquidity risks and the policy it will follow to address such risks, and the results of this hypothetical simulation, to assess the policy it followed in this regards and determine methods for its development.

Structured Product: a security or other asset resulting from a securitization transaction or scheme or similar structure.

Subsidiary: in relation to a company, another company which it controls.

Subordinated Loans: the loans with conditions stating that in the event of liquidation or bankruptcy, the principal of the loans and its interest, shall not be paid until all other creditors have been paid in full.Art. 1(f), Prudential Rules

Substantial Shareholder: a person holding

(5%) or more of the class of shares of the issuer or voting rights therein. Art 1., Corporate Governance Regulations

Substantial Unitholder: means in the Investment Funds Regulations and the Real Estate Investment Funds Regulations, a person who owns 5% or more of the units of a closed- ended investment traded fund or a real estate investment traded fund.

Suit: the complaint filed with the Committee starting from submitting it in a written Statement of Claim according to the Securities Dispute regulations until the suit is closed by a final decision.Art. 1, Securities Disputes Proceedings Regulations

Suitability Report: The report prepared in accordance with the requirements of paragraph (c) of Article 43 of the Capital Market Institutions Regulations.

Swap Agreements: an agreement for the benefit of a foreign counterparts to transfer the economic benefits of securities listed on the Exchange to those foreign investors through swap transactions. Art.1, Circular 5/2132

U

Ultimate Beneficiary: a non-resident foreign investor that receives the economic benefits of the securities listed on the Saudi Stock Exchange through swap transactions executed under the Swap Agreements. Question 63, QFI FAQ.

Unconditional as to Acceptances: means in the Merger and Acquisition Regulations, that the offer is no longer conditional upon receipt by the offeror of acceptances from the shareholders of the offeree company.

Underwriter: a person who buys securities from the issuer or an affiliate of the issuer for the purpose of offering, placing and marketing such securities to the public, or a person who sells securities on behalf of the issuer or an affiliate of the issuer for the purpose of making a public offering and placement of such securities. Relatives: husband, wife and minor children. Art. 1, Capital Markets Law

Unit: the share of any owner in any fund consisting of units or a part of it. Each unit shall be

W

Warrant: warrants and other instruments entitling the holder to subscribe for any shares or debt instruments.

Wrong-Way Risk: the risk arising from exposure to a counterparty when the collateral provided by that counterparty is highly correlated with the credit quality of that counterparty. Article 2, Securities Central Counterparts Regulations.

X Y Z

[Reserved]

CATALOG OF SAUDI SECURITIES LAWS

Investment Funds Regulations

IPO Book Building

IPO Price Stabilization Mechanism

Joint Stock Companies Companies Regulatory Rules, Procedures and Guidance Note

Market Conduct Regulations

Merger and Acquisition Regulations

Non-Resident Foreigners Investment in Parallel Market Guidance Note

Offers of Securities Regulations

Procedures for Listed Companies with Losses

Prudential Rules

Public Consultations on Implementing Regulations

Qualified Foreign Financial Institutions Regulations

Real Estate Investment Funds Regulations

Registration of Auditors

Securities Borrowing and Lending Regulations

Securities Disputes

Short Selling Regulations

Securities Central Counterparties Regulations

Special Purpose Entities Rules

Swap Agreements Framework

NOTES

Introduction

1. Issued by the Board of the Capital Market Authority pursuant to its Resolution Number 4-11-2004 Dated 20/8/1425 H.(4/10/2004 G.), based on the Capital Market Law issued by Royal Decree No. M/30 dated 2/6/1424 H., as amended by Resolution of the Board of the Capital Market Authority Number 2-22-2021 dated 12/7/1442 H. (24/2/2021 G.)

ABOUT THE AUTHOR

Michael O'Kane is an attorney with two decades' experience in Saudi Arabia and the Middle East. He is a former special legal advisor to the Kingdom of Saudi Arabia and in that capacity drafted a legal code for the Kingdom's Economic Cities project. He advised the Saudi Railways Commission and assisted them in drafting regulations. He advised KA-CARE, the King Abdullah City for Atomic and Renewable Energy in drafting a law for the peaceful use of nuclear energy in the Kingdom. His book, *Doing Business in Saudi Arabia* is on Amazon's International Law bestseller list. He has published *Saudi Securities Law, Saudi Labor Law Outline; Saudi Real Estate Law* and *Law and Rockets: An American Lawyer in Iraq.*

He may be contacted at mok@mu7ami.com.

🐦 twitter.com/al_mu7ami